Hummingbirds

Hummingbirds

JEWELS ON AIR

by

Melanie Votaw

COURAGE BOOKS

AN IMPRINT OF RUNNING PRESS
PHILADELPHIA • LONDON

9 8 7 6 5 4 3 2 1
Digit on the right indicates the number of this printing
Library of Congress Cataloging-in-Publication Number 2002108143
ISBN 0-7624-1494-4
Photo research by Susan Oyama
Designed by Serrin Bodmer
Edited by Susan K. Hom
Typography: Garamond 3, Veljovic, and Monkton
This book may be ordered by mail from the publisher.
But try your bookstore first!
Published by Courage Books, an imprint of Running Press Book Publishers
125 South Twenty-second Street
Philadelphia, Pennsylvania 19103-4399
Visit us on the web!
www.runningpress.com

CONTENTS

PART ONE:

The Miracle of Hummingbirds

"Where do passions find room in so diminutive a body?"
—HECTOR ST. JOHN DE CRÈVECOEUR

fter an eternity at sea, an early European explorer and his crew step into a strange new world. Their senses are overwhelmed with scents and sounds unlike any they have ever experienced. Peculiar trees, flowers, and creatures surround them in all directions. But nothing can prepare them for the enormous insect that passes through their peripheral vision. As they turn and focus their eyes, they are astonished that this insect has . . . *feathers?* Speechless, they watch as it darts out of sight.

Was it a fairy? An angel perhaps? It was too large to be an insect. Too small to be a bird. If they dare tell of the "insect bird," will anyone believe them, or simply accuse them of suffering from some exotic fever?

Even though Columbus wrote of hummingbirds in his diaries, early Europeans did not believe the first explorers' tales of a bird that flies like an insect. In time, as more and more eyewitness accounts reached the continent, the bird named for the sound of its lightning fast wings captured the European imagination. For centuries, indigenous peoples had considered hummingbirds to be magical. Their oral traditions, as well as the early written accounts in Europe, proved what is still true today—it is impossible to describe hummingbirds without using superlatives.

With the most rapid wing-beats of all birds—up to 200 per second—hummingbirds certainly live in the fast lane. Yet, they are the smallest birds in the world, equivalent in size to a human thumb and weighing no more than a penny. In fact, some dragonflies are larger! For a pound of hummingbirds, you would need to collect at least 150 of them.

By human standards, hummingbirds are confirmed sugar addicts. They can drink the nectar from as many as 3,000 flowers a day, consuming up to 75 percent of their body weight.

RIGHT: This male blue-throated hummingbird (Lampornis clemenciae) *at Miller Canyon, Arizona displays his blue throat and black tail with white tips.*

You would have to eat 20,000 calories daily or 50 pounds of sugar to keep pace with just one hummingbird.

Hummers, as they are lovingly called by bird watchers, are the air show of the avian world. They can fly in any direction, including backwards, and can hover in midair, their wings nothing more than a blur to the human eye.

The hummingbird's infinitesimal heart equals more than two percent of its total body weight, is eight times faster than the human heart, and is proportionately larger than the heart of any other warm blooded animal on earth.

Its brain is comparatively larger than other birds, though still only the size of a pea. While our human brain equals only two percent of our weight, a hummingbird's brain accounts for more than four percent of its weight. With a phenomenal memory and well-known intelligence, its cranial cavity may be pea sized, but the hummingbird is certainly no birdbrain!

Despite their improbable size, both male and female hummers are fierce and fearless, and have no qualms about jousting with any adversary (including humans) if food is at stake.

As if all of this were not enough, hummingbird feathers are so beautiful that John James Audubon called the birds "glittering fragments of the rainbow." The males of most species sport iridescent colors that can suddenly change with the direction of the sun. Elusive reds, greens, purples, or blues are one moment brilliant, and the next, dull blacks or

HUMMINGBIRD FACTS:

- Even though the hummingbird's brain is the size of a pea, it is comparatively larger than the human brain.

- A hummingbird weighs no more than three paper clips.

- Translating a hummingbird's metabolism into human terms would require you eat nearly 300 pounds of hamburger each day just to maintain your body weight.

- Hummingbirds breathe more than four times per second *while resting*.

- Hummingbird wingbeats span from 50 per second to as high as 200 per second.

LEFT: A male violet-tailed sylph (Aglaiocercus coelestis) *rests in Bellavista, Ecuador. Like all hummingbirds, his tiny feet are useful for little more than holding onto branches. He must lift off in flight just to turn around on the branch. This species is particularly well-known for the male's exceptionally long violet tail feathers.*

grays. A blaze of color bright as neon can flash with a simple turn of the bird's head.

Such is the miracle of the hummingbird.

That humankind has long been enamored with hummingbirds is obvious in the poetic names given to the various species, such as "brilliant," "emerald," "comet," "sunangel," "mango," "coquette," "starfrontlet," and "mountain-gem."

The continents of Asia, Africa, Australia, and Europe can claim myriad exotic birds, but they are all bereft of hummingbirds. Only North and South America can boast these amazing creations. With over 340 known species, there are more different kinds of hummingbirds than any other type of bird in the Americas, except for fly-

catchers, with about 360 species. Only 16 hummingbird species breed in North America, however, with a handful of vagrants occasionally making their way north during the summer. Forty-nine of the United States will be visited by at least one species of hummingbird during the summer months, if not year round. Hawaii is the only state devoid of them.

Surprisingly, hummingbirds exist from Alaska to the islands off the southern tip of South America in habitats as diverse as tropical forests, deserts, and the cold mountaintops of the Andes.

Even though there remain many unsolved mysteries about these birds, much is now known about their anatomy and habits, proving that hummingbirds are a glowing example of nature's perfection. If they were any larger, they would not be able to hover, and if they were any smaller, they would not be able to eat enough to maintain their necessary high energy. Therefore, the greatest miracle about hummingbirds is that they manage to survive at all.

AERODYNAMIC WONDERS

While scientists understand how the hummingbird's unique anatomy enables its aerial feats, even our most impressive Top Gun maneuvers fail to come close. Helicopters are our nearest mechanical imitators, but they are inept and awkward by comparison.

A quick tilt of the wings, and hummingbirds can change direction in an instant. They are the only birds that can fly in all directions, including sideways, backward, and upside down. They have even been caught performing backward somersaults when startled. However, it is their ability to hover that fascinates us most. *How do they do it?*

Flight is possible for birds largely because of strong but very light bones that are mostly hollow. These bones actually

ABOVE: A male white-vented plumeleteer (Chalybura buffonii) in Panama shows off the amazing aerodynamic feats of the hummingbird. Named for the white feathers in the vent under its tail, the plumeleteer is highly territorial and twitters noisily when defending its food sources.

weigh two to three times less than their feathers. The wings of most birds flex during flight and are constructed with long arm bones and short finger bones. Hummingbird wings are the opposite, with short arm bones and long finger bones that allow them to flex only at the shoulder. While this may seem to be a disadvantage, a ball and socket joint at the shoulder allows for a nearly 180 degree rotation of the wings. Hovering is possible because of this unique ability to rotate their long, tapered wings vertically, as well as horizontally, in a small but rapid figure eight movement.

If you imagine your arm as similar to the bone structure of a hummingbird wing, you would not be able to bend at the elbow or wrist, your fingers would comprise most of the length of your arm, and you would be able to turn your shoulder almost all the way around. This construction affords the hummer a command of the air beyond that of any other bird.

While human chest muscles make up about five percent of our total body weight, a hummingbird's chest and flight muscles account for one-quarter of its weight. A deep sternum and two more ribs than other birds hold the exceptionally powerful muscles to the tiny skeleton. These flight muscles allow it to obtain lift in the air whether its wings are flapping up or down.

ABOVE TOP: The red throat feathers of the male calliope hummingbird (Stellula calliope), *pictured here in Tucson, Arizona, streak down the sides of his neck.*

ABOVE BOTTOM: Known for his bright red-orange gorget, the male ruby-topaz hummingbird (Chrysolampis mosquitus) *fans his orange tail on the island of Tobago in the West Indies.*

ABOVE: *The rufous hummingbird* (Selasphorus rufus) *of the western United States is well-known for its strong personality. Both males and females will chase away insects, as well as other birds, to protect precious flowers and feeders.*

RIGHT: *A female black-throated mango* (Anthracothorax nigricollis) *extends her tongue at a feeder on Tobago. While she is not as brightly colored as the male of her species, pictured on page 79, she sports an unusual black vertical stripe down her white belly.*

ABOVE: If you see a hummingbird without a red gorget in the northeastern United States, chances are it is a female ruby-throated hummingbird (Archilochus colubris), *as this is the only species which breeds in the northeast. Immature males with undeveloped gorgets are sometimes mistaken for females, however.*

Other species of birds can only gain lift on the downward stroke, and then drop a little during the upward stroke.

Add to this the hummingbird's ability to flap its wings at up to 80 beats per second during normal flight and as much as 200 beats per second during a speed dive maneuver, and you truly have an amazing flying machine. By comparison, most small birds beat their wings at less than 30 beats per second. Backward and upside down flight can be achieved only for short distances, while hovering requires such a costly expenditure of energy that it is used as sparingly as possible. Still, if you observe a hummingbird while feeding, it appears to be hovering and flying backward quite frequently. Its tail fans out, bobs up and down, and serves as a brake during quick stops in midair. It hovers at a flower or feeder, sips the nectar, and then flies backward to hover briefly before sipping again.

Hummers, like all other flying birds, have a uniquely efficient respiratory system. Unlike human lungs, a bird's respiratory system provides a continuous influx of air and includes air sacs, which are extensions of the lungs. Hummingbirds once again have been given a little extra, with nine air sacs, compared to the six belonging to most birds. Because of the enormous amount of energy needed for hovering, the extra air sacs make absolute evolutionary sense.

While hummingbirds are clearly built for flight, they are not the fastest distance fliers in the avian world. Still, for their size, it is remarkable that some species have been clocked in wind tunnels at forward speeds of 40 miles per hour.

The miniature feet of hummingbirds are very weak in comparison to their muscular bodies and can only be used for gripping branches and grooming feathers. Even when they want to turn around on a branch, they must lift off in flight to move. However, no takeoff is necessary. Three swift wing flaps is all it takes to be up from a perch at full power, returning for an absolutely seamless landing.

BELOW: The male ruby-throated hummingbird (Archilochus colubris) *is unmistakable with his bright red gorget, green crown, white belly, and slightly forked tail.*

FLASHY FEATHERS

BELOW TOP: Typical of many male hummingbird species, the gorget of this male rufous hummingbird (Selasphorus rufus) *is dull in color when turned away from the light.*

BELOW BOTTOM: When the male rufous (Selasphorus rufus) *faces the sunlight, his gorget shines in all its coppery glory.*

Feathers are without a doubt one of nature's most amazing inventions. They are strong, yet light and waterproof, and keep birds insulated from the cold. The iridescent feathers of the hummingbird, however, take the invention one step further.

The majority of the colors we see everyday are created by pigments. This includes the feathers of most birds, as well as the rusty brown color on some hummingbirds, such as the rufous hummingbird.

Pigmented feathers can be seen regardless of the lighting, while the iridescence of hummingbird feathers can only be seen when light strikes them. This is why many hummingbird feathers will appear vivid one moment, yet dull and colorless the next.

The scientific explanation for how hummingbird feathers work is extremely technical. The process, which has been named interference, is similar to that which creates a rainbow in a soap bubble. The feathers are constructed of microscopic "barbules," which contain color disks called platelets. Inside the platelets are air bubbles

ABOVE: *It is easy to see how the male magnificent hummingbird* (Eugenes fulgens) *of southwestern North America got his name, with his bright green gorget, violet-blue crown, and dark body. In dull lighting, he appears solid black, earning him the nickname, "Black Knight."*

and layers of melanin, the thickness of which determine the color of the feather. If the barbules, which reflect as mirrors, are densely stacked together, the color and iridescence will be especially intense. Most hummingbirds have iridescent green backs, which can be seen in any light. In this case, the barbules reflect in all directions. In the case of feathers that change color depending upon the light, the barbules only reflect in one direction. Only the bottom third of such feathers are iridescent, but because they are so tightly layered over one another, they appear to produce endless color.

Females tend to have slightly larger bodies and bills, but it is the males that dazzle with the vibrant hues that have made hummingbirds famous. While the males and females of some species, such as the hermits, are indistinguishable from one another, most hummingbirds have dimorphic plumage, which means that the sexes do not look alike. The females may seem drab by comparison, but their duller colors keep them safer from predators while nesting.

ABOVE: *This timid male violet-bellied hummingbird* (Damophila julie), *pictured at the Canopy Tower in Panama, steals a few sips from a feeder before being chased away by more aggressive species.*

One of the most colorful parts of a male hummingbird is the throat and chin, which is called the gorget. This is the area that most often changes color, suddenly blazing with the intensity of a flashlight. At the Asa Wright Nature Centre in Trinidad, the appearance of the ruby-topaz hummingbird always causes a stir. Everyone keeps his or her binoculars glued to the bird on its perch, waiting for his head to turn. Depending upon the angle, they are rewarded with a flare of orange or red. The gorget is best seen when the light is shining on the bird and shining behind the observer.

The forehead and crown of the male hummer, collectively called the helmet, is also often brilliantly colored.

To a large degree, the male hummingbird can control how his feathers appear. He may cause his gorget feathers to flare out and sparkle in order to announce his presence to an attractive female. He knows exactly how to move his feathers in relation to the sun to achieve the flashiest effect or to virtually disappear in the presence of a predator.

Hummingbirds may be tiny, but their feathers are more numerous per skin area than on any other bird, even though the total number of feathers is only about 1,000, compared with a swan's 25,000.

FOOD AT A HEARTBEAT

It may seem ironic that the world's smallest bird is the one most preoccupied with food, but its miniature size is precisely what makes this obsession necessary. With the fastest metabolism of all vertebrates, a hummingbird could die within a day if it fails to take in more energy than it loses.

Just as a military jet requires a great deal of fuel to maneuver, so does the hummingbird. Nectar is digested within an hour, and 97 percent of it is immediately converted into energy. The only way a hummingbird can maintain its metabolism is to eat approximately every ten minutes. This explains why it never seems to be still. Its heart beats more than 20 times per second, expending energy at an intense pace, sometimes feeding and urinating at the same time. Even at rest, it breathes as much as 250 times per minute. Despite its fast digestion, the bird must wait a few minutes for the food in its crop to move into its digestive system before consuming more. Therefore, contrary to

OPPOSITE PAGE: A green hermit (Phaethornis guy) samples a poro flower in Costa Rica, showing off his blue rump and two long white tail feathers.

popular belief, 80 percent of a hummer's time is spent at rest.

Hummingbirds require flowers for sustenance, and flowers require hummingbirds to pollinate them. This remarkable synchronous relationship is a process called coevolution or coadaptation. "Ornithophilous," which literally means "bird lovers," is the name given to flowers which require pollination by birds. Hummingbird flowers typically bloom during the day, are vividly colored, often tubular shaped, and contain abundant nectar, but no scent. Since hummingbirds have excellent color vision but no sense of smell, coupled with long, narrow bills, these flowers are literally designed for them.

FEATHER FACTS:

When the anatomy of the hummingbird feather meets with light, the result is brilliant iridescent color. Just as the spectrum of a soap bubble or rainbow change depending upon the direction of light, the colors of a male hummingbird can change with a quick turn of the head. Females are more dully colored to keep them safe from predators while nesting, and immature males are often mistaken for females before they develop their telltale flash and flare.

LEFT: A male violet sabrewing (Campylopterus hemileucurus) *fans his white-tipped tail as he hovers at the yellow flowers of justice in Costa Rica. Though violet in front, his back is dark green.*

Nature is exceptionally creative in devising ways to reduce competition between animals for nectar. Flowers bloom at different times to ensure that none are neglected. They have evolved to specialize in certain animals, just as animals have evolved to specialize in certain flowers. Insects see the color blue better than red and also use their sense of smell when choosing flowers. Bees prefer higher concentrations of sugar than hummingbirds, which favor nectars averaging only 25 percent sugar. Bats feed on nectar and pollinate some plants, but are exactly opposite to hummingbirds, in that they have an excellent sense of smell and poor vision. Bats are likely, therefore, to pollinate scented white flowers easily found at night. Without

long bills, insects and bats cannot feed from long tubular flowers, nor can they easily hover and feed at the same time. Insects must land somewhere on the flower in order to feed. Flowers that have no landing area can only be frequented by hummingbirds. Although to conserve energy, hummers will perch to feed whenever possible. Flowers at high elevations are especially in need of hummingbirds to pollinate them, as insects have difficulty surviving the colder climate at these altitudes.

Every time a hummingbird sips nectar, the flower's anther brushes pollen onto the bird's body. When the bird probes its next dozen or so blossoms, the flower's stigma brushes the pollen off the bird, allowing the plant to reproduce. In perhaps the most

ABOVE: A male tufted coquette (Lophornis ornatus) licks the air with his long stretchy tongue. The smallest bird on Trinidad and Tobago, he measures only 2³/₄ inches from beak to tail. Because of his dramatic red "punk rock" head feathers and neck tufts, he is very sought after by bird watchers.

amazing example of coevolution, humming-bird flowers have adapted the location of their anthers so that they leave pollen on different parts of the bird's body—either the forehead, crown or bill. When the hummingbird visits the same type of flower, the stigma will be properly positioned to brush the pollen from the bird. This prevents the specialized pollens from being wasted on the wrong flower. Coevolution is a continuous process, and researchers who study the same species of flowers and birds for periods of years can observe it gradually taking place before their eyes.

To spend as little fuel as possible while searching for food, nature has endowed hummingbirds with an extraordinary memory. They instinctively gravitate back to sites of previously gratifying meals, thus saving valuable energy. Even though the birds have learned that red flowers are generally rewarding, research has shown that they are perfectly content feeding from a flower of most any color as long as it literally "fits the bill" and has an optimal gift of nectar. Since their memories tell them red flowers have been worthwhile, they may attempt to feed from any number of red objects, including the floral fabric of a blouse, in the hopes of revisiting the sweet prize. If they make a mistake, they will not repeat the error.

PREVIOUS PAGE: A female Anna's hummingbird (Calypte anna) *of the western United States probes a tubular flower. Unlike the female ruby-throated, female Anna's usually have a few sparse red throat feathers.*

Hummingbirds have two feeding styles. Some species are territorial and feed from a small area which they guard and protect. Some even feed from only one type of plant, which they must defend vehemently from others of their species.

The other feeding style is called traplining, a term borrowed from fur trappers who laid traps in a line. These species feed buffet style, traveling from flower to flower in a patterned line that covers more terrain than territorial birds. They feed from the outer reaches of their territory first, depleting the flowers in order to discourage intruders from the interior. Some South American species spend the day feeding from flowers up and down the side of a mountain. Trapliners have developed exceptional strength for flying distances and tend to drink from a greater variety of flowers,

ABOVE: A fiery-throated hummingbird (Panterpe insignis) *sips from a heliconia in the Costa Rican cloudforest. Note the white spot behind the eye. In bright sunlight, the gorget is orange surrounded by yellow.*

which are decided survival advantages. If necessary, however, territorial hummers will trapline, and vice versa.

The hummingbird's long and tapered bill is perfectly constructed for probing deep into flowers for nectar, especially blossoms with a tubular shape. The bill is made of a material similar to the horn of an antelope and is generally brown or black in color, although some species sport bright red bills. Unlike other birds, the top portion of the bill overlaps the bottom portion, fitting together like a box.

Bill sizes and shapes vary from species to species, causing them to specialize in certain flowers. Additionally, mountain species will inhabit different elevations, while forest species will feed at different levels of the rainforest from the forest floor to the canopy, never even crossing paths with one another.

The hummer's tongue, with approximately 50 taste buds

along its length, is translucent and somewhat stretchy. It can extend beyond the length of the bill to lick nectar at the ravenous pace of twelve licks or more per second. This stretch is possible because the tongue is attached to tissue that literally unwinds to extend and rewinds at the back of the throat when the bird is at rest. The action of capillaries in the tongue moves the nectar into the bird's mouth. In addition, some species have brushlike tongues that are grooved or fringed on the sides with a tiny fork at the tip. This ingenious design helps to hold more nectar on the tongue, allowing for greater licking speed.

While it is commonly believed hummingbirds need high amounts of nectar to survive, they can actually subsist largely on insects. Insects provide necessary daily protein, and one hummer can partake of more than 600 in a single day, digesting each meal in ten minutes. Hummingbirds will consume any insect small enough to swallow, including ants, caterpillars, mosquitoes, gnats, aphids, fruit flies, and larvae.

Clutching them in their bills, the birds will "hawk" insects in mid-flight and often gorge themselves in a swarm. Despite their champion flight techniques, hummingbirds are less efficient predators than flycatchers, but still maintain an enviable success rate. Some espouse the theory that hummingbirds may be able to control the movement of air from their wings to such a degree that they can prevent insects from flying out of their clutches and even draw insects into their mouths.

"Gleaning" is a simpler way to eat insects and insect eggs by picking them off plants and trees. In another use of wing wind, hummers have been observed flying close to the ground

in order to turn leaves over and expose the insects underneath.

TINY, BRAVE SPEED DEMONS

Don't let the sweet appearance of hummingbirds fool you. Early accounts described them as fighting "like lions." If you remain near their food sources for any length of time, be prepared for chirps of complaint or a blur of wings whizzing past your nose in a clear message to step away from the flowers or feeders. You might also expect to find a hummingbird hovering inches in front of your face, staring you down without the slightest hint of fear. While hummers can sometimes be shy, their speed and unmatched agility make them virtually fearless, ready and willing to take on any adversary that gets in their way, from tiny insect to giant human. They do occasionally dive-bomb people, but there is no documented case of anyone being injured by a hummingbird.

The occasional "snap" or "thud" heard near a group of hummers feeding together is most certainly the sound of two birds crashing together in the air. To protect their established food sources, they kick their claws at one another in mid-flight. One may dive-bomb another, locking bills with it and circling to the ground. They rarely hurt one another in these bouts, but one bird may

PREVIOUS PAGE: In South America, two shining sunbeam hummingbirds (Aglaeactis cupripennis) battle over territory.

win the territory of another. Hardly the tender animals of the imagination, adult hummers only touch each other when mating or fighting.

Hummingbirds need to take in food frequently so they cannot afford to be generous. Their vigorous jousting is not generally for sport. However, buff-bellied hummingbirds in the southeastern United States have been observed temporarily abandoning their own plentiful territories to noisily invade the territories of others as if simply for fun.

Before resorting to combat, hummingbirds will try to deter intruders with vocalized warnings and chases. Some species, such as Anna's hummingbirds, puff their feathers in an attempt to look larger and more menacing. Fight behavior appears to be instinctive, as chicks begin showing aggression just days after leaving the nest.

At the Asa Wright Nature Centre in Trinidad, the white-chested emerald is "king of the feeders" and often collides with the white-necked jacobins that also frequent the Centre. White-chested emeralds have even been seen chasing away hawks, demonstrating that small size can be

TOP: A male white-necked jacobin (Florisuga mellivora) displays the white spot on the back of his neck, deep blue crown, and spectacular front wing position while hovering at a feeder at the Asa Wright Nature Centre in Trinidad.

BOTTOM: The front view of this male white-necked jacobin (Florisuga mellivora) in Panama shows his white belly, topped with a blue and green tuxedo-like gorget and chest.

ABOVE: A male violet-crowned hummingbird (Amazilia violiceps) *in Mexico displays his violet crown and red bill while tending to the care and maintenance of his feathers.*

BELOW: A Brazilian ruby (Clytolaema rubricauda) *takes a break from feeding for a belly wiggle in some water. Frequent bathing is necessary to keep feathers in optimal condition.*

an advantage in combat. For the hawk, it is akin to being pierced repeatedly with a needle that cannot be caught.

A TYPICAL WORK DAY

A hummingbird's day generally begins at dawn. After some stretching, the bird will need to eat right away in order to make up for the energy lost during the night. A hummingbird will spend the majority of its day at rest, but only for short periods of time. Feeding will take place up to fifteen times per hour, and the remainder of the hour will be spent perched. Sitting is rarely idle, however, as this time is needed for digestion and preening. Feathers must be groomed frequently by stretching, wiggling, shaking, and stroking.

A territorial hummer will keep its eyes almost incessantly on its chosen flowers or feeders, ready to rise from

its perch to defend them. The bird will return time and again to the same perch, only occasionally resting elsewhere. Trapliners, on the other hand, will travel from flower to flower, stopping to rest at various perches along the way.

In order to keep feathers in optimal condition, bathing is a crucial job that must be done several times a day. A birdbath or any small pool of standing water will suffice, as the hummingbird wiggles its belly and chin in the water for a good splash. It may also stand and allow water to roll from its head to its back. Showers are preferable, though, and standing with feathers fluffed in a light rainfall is perfection, as is a flight through a small waterfall, sprinkler, or even a garden hose.

Of course, bathing tends to muss feathers. Preening, therefore, is a necessity after a bath. Both bill and claw perform this task expertly, extracting oil from a gland near the tail. The oil is much like a waxy polish which not only keeps feathers beautiful and properly placed, but removes dust and mites. Each feather is carefully stroked, as survival requires them to be kept in top working order. The head and neck feathers can only be reached by the claws, which serve as a comb. The bill is easily wiped clean of sticky nectar and pollen with the stroke of a claw or a rub against a branch.

The hummingbird's day ends with dusk, after gorging itself in order to store enough energy to make it through the night without feeding. Without this energy storage, it would die of hypothermia, making sleep a dangerous undertaking. However, it has an uncanny ability to control its body temperature, even during the long night. If the night is warm and there has been plenty of food to eat, the bird will be able to sleep normally. If the night has been cold or food has been too scarce to store enough energy, the bird will go into a coma-like state called torpor, which is similar to hibernation.

TORPOR FACTS:

If you find a "dead" hummingbird perched on a branch, think again! He's probably pulling a Rip Van Winkle. In order to survive without feeding overnight, hummingbirds often go into a torpid state of sleep to conserve energy. They intentionally lower their body temperature and slow their heart rate so much that they cannot be roused until their temperature and heart rate rise again.

Torpor is nature's way of making up for the lack of downy under-feathers possessed by most birds. While it may seem an evolutionary mistake to deny hummers this extra layer, they cannot sweat and must cool down by panting during rest to release heat and inhale oxygen. Therefore, the added layer of down would not only add too much weight, but might cause the birds to overheat during their extraordinarily active day.

The lower a hummingbird's body temperature can safely go during the night, the less energy it will expend. In the torpid state, the normal 105 degree Fahrenheit body temperature can drop below 50 degrees. Some reports claim the heart rate can slow to less than 40 beats per minute from the average of 1,000 or more during the day. Minutes may pass without a single breath, and the bird will appear to be dead. People have lifted a supposedly dead hummingbird from a branch only to find it awakening and flying away a few hours later.

Although torpor is occasionally spent upside down on a perch, the bird will generally sleep upright with its neck withdrawn somewhat into its body and its bill pointed straight up to the sky. It relaxes and fluffs its feathers to release body heat, and in less than an hour slows down its lightning metabolism enough for torpid sleep.

Instinctive conservationists, hummingbirds will break the rule of awakening at dawn if they need to save more energy, sometimes remaining in the torpid state for as long as 14 hours. Coming out of this deep sleep is not easy and takes some time to raise the body temperature enough for movement. Studies have shown that hummers cannot fly until their body temperature has risen to at least 86 degrees Fahrenheit.

Torpor is what allows mountain hummingbirds to survive in cold altitudes of up to 15,000 feet above sea level. In the Andes of South America, they roost in caves during the night and go into torpor as the air temperature falls.

Of course, illness or excessive cold can disturb a hummer's ability to control its body temperature, causing it to perish during sleep. Is there any doubt that hummingbirds live on the edge?

Do Hummingbirds Sing?

Hummingbirds do indeed sing, although they are hardly the most melodic members of the avian world, as they lack the strong vocal muscles of songbirds. With such amazing attributes as wings that hum, it would seem greedy to expect them to possess exceptional singing ability.

Yet, these tiny beings make a number of calls that differ from species to species. Some observers insist that a few, such as the wedge-tailed sabrewing of Central America, have beautiful and varied songs. Some species chant a single note, while others vocalize with throaty sounds, chirps and chatter, which become louder and faster when defending territory or attracting a mate.

The rufous hummingbird makes a clicking sound, while the broad-billed hummingbird produces a rasp. The Allen's hummingbird trills its song, and the white-eared hummingbird's song sounds much like a bell. The Anna's hummingbird is famous for its vocalizations during courtship. For assistance in identifying different species, recordings of their songs can be found on various Internet websites.

The most famous singing hummingbirds are the less colorful hermits, which reside in the tropics. Males congregate in groups which are called *leks* and vocalize together to attract females for mating. Birds of other species, such as manakins, also create leks for this purpose.

LOVE AND MARRIAGE

The way to a hummingbird's heart is through its stomach, as the hummer is faithful only to food sources. Hardly romantic, the constant competition for food necessitates a solitary life.

Males will mate with as many females as possible during the breeding season, expending a great deal of energy and body fat in the process. Females will sometimes mate and lay eggs more than once, although it is rare to lay more than two sets of eggs per season. Both sexes begin mating at about one year old.

ABOVE: There's no question why this bird (Microchera albocoronata) is called the snowcap hummingbird, as it hovers in the Costa Rican rainforest.

OPPOSITE PAGE: The highly territorial male rufous hummingbird (Selasphorus rufus) poses for a portrait in Nutrioso, Arizona. The rufous migrates the longest distance of any hummingbird. Rufous populations have been steadily declining over the last several years.

ABOVE: The extension of the red gorget along the sides of the neck is clear in this photo of a male Anna's hummingbird (Calypte anna), *as it tastes the nectar of a Cape Honeysuckle flower. This species is common west of the Sierras on the west coast of the United States.*

The female usually begins the process by approaching the male's feeding territory. He may treat her as an intruder at first and try to chase her from his food sources. When she responds to his aggression passively by flying away, he chases her into neutral territory that has neither been established for feeding or nesting, where he will perform his courtship displays.

These courtship rituals can be very entertaining and are often indistinguishable from fighting displays. To attract the female who has captured his attention, the male may flash and flare his gorget feathers, vocalize loudly, and move his head swiftly back and forth, much the same as he would try to frighten away a food competitor.

Courtship flights vary from species to species and can take the form of a U, J, or O-shaped dive accompanied by wing sounds and song. The Anna's hummingbird flies high, and then dives down near the female in a swooping motion, making a sound with the feathers of his tail. The Costa's hummingbird whistles during his courtship dance. Some species, like the ruby-throated hummingbird, perform "shuttle flights," swooping from side to side like a hypnotist's watch. The female indeed seems to go into an altered state, remaining still except to gaze back and forth at his flight as if viewing a tennis match. His swoops become shorter and closer to her until he mounts her. A Peruvian species called

ABOVE: The white-chested emerald (Amazilia chionopectus) *is Trinidad's most aggressive hummingbird. A vehement protector of its territory, it is frequently seen (and heard) kicking other humming-* *birds in mid-air. The emerald lacks the bright colors of many other species, but iridescent yellow and green feathers on the sides of the neck and chest can be seen in bright light.*

the spatuletail has a particularly unique performance, raising the round circles at the end of his thin tail feathers around his face.

In the dark, shaded tropical forests, the male hermit hummingbirds lack the flashy colors with which to attract females. Instead, a group of as many as one hundred males gather in a lek and sing together in a seductive choir. The same lek sites, on the ground or in trees, are often used year after year. In Trinidad, little hermits may sing the same song over and over 12,000 times a day for nine months of the year.

Intercourse between hummingbirds lasts from two to five seconds, but in the fast pace of a hummingbird's life, perhaps this is long enough. Females have even been observed hanging upside down on a perch during a sexual encounter. After mating, the two will separate almost immediately, and the female will not tolerate the male in her nesting territory. Male hummingbirds do not in any way participate in the care of offspring. There are rare accounts of males incubating or feeding young, but researchers find these reports to be highly suspect.

Hormones trigger females to begin work on their nests even before they've located a mate. This process can take up to two weeks, unless she is rebuilding a nest built in a previous breeding season. The nesting territory is aggressively protected against any potential threats, including other hummingbirds of both sexes.

Most hummingbird nests are smaller than a baseball on the outside, with the smallest nests barely large enough on the inside to hold a nickel. The female will use whatever materials are available in her habitat, which can consist of lichens, bark, moss, leaves, fur, feathers, caterpillar silk, and even cloth or dryer lint. You might even find a brave female stealing thread from your back or hair from your head.

Several thousands of miles of spider web silk are most frequently used to hold it all together like glue. This is ingenious, as there is believed to be no stronger substance in nature than spider silk, and scientists have yet to replicate it in the laboratory.

The cleverly constructed nests are a lesson in camouflage, as they always blend with their habitat. The female works painstakingly to make her home durable on the outside and lined with cushiony, insulated materials on the inside. She uses her bill like a tweezer or sewing needle to weave the nest, molding it to the shape of her body, and packing it tightly with her feet.

BELOW: A female little hermit (Phaethornis longuemareus) *builds her pendulous nest on the edges of a leaf in the Trinidad rainforest. The nest is stronger than it looks and safely out of the reach of most predators.*

ABOVE: *A female*
broad-billed hummingbird
(Cynanthus latirostris)
incubates her eggs in Madera
Canyon, Arizona. She has
molded the cup-shaped nest
to her body and arches her
back so that her tail extends
out. While some cup nests
are perfectly round, this one
extends downward to hold
it securely to the tree.

All North American species build cup shaped nests, but some South American species, especially hermits, build pendulous nests that hang precariously by a thread from a leaf or branch, out of the reach of predatory snakes. The bottom of the nests is counterweighted, and they are often built under a leaf, which serves as an umbrella or roof. Some hummer architects living in areas with exceptionally high rainfall even construct nests that can withstand rain passing through them.

After mating, the eggs only take a couple of days to develop in the female's body. All hummingbirds lay two white eggs separately a day or two apart. Even though the eggs are only about half the size of a jellybean, they can amount to almost 20 percent of the female's weight, equivalent to a 20-pound human baby.

Not surprisingly, breeding season occurs when the most flowers are blooming. With ample food available, the mother will feed close to her nest and as little as possible, leaving her more time to sit on her nest. She eats most just before dusk so that she can maintain her metabolism during the night without having to go into torpor. Since chicks cannot control their body temperature and must rely on their mother to keep them warm, only a brooding female in the Andes or other extreme circumstances will enter the torpid state during the night, as her lower body temperature could threaten her young.

Incubation is not just a process of warming the eggs and chicks, but also cooling them from too much sunlight. When necessary, the female will turn the eggs with her bill to maintain the correct temperature. The chicks are born blind, have no feathers, and are silent, even when fed, which appears to keep them safer from predators. A temporary tooth on their bills, coupled with a strong muscle on the back of their heads,

assist them in getting "out of their shells," and they don't open their eyes until their second week.

The mother hummingbird eats mostly insects mixed with just a little nectar, which she half digests and regurgitates into the hungry mouths of her young. About three times per hour, her throat swells to pump the food to the tip of her bill, which she moves up and down in the throats of her chicks similar to a sewing machine needle. To human eyes, it appears that her bill dips uncomfortably all the way into the chick's body. As the chicks grow, the mother will increase the amount of nectar and reduce the number of insects in the regurgitated food.

Researchers estimate that as few as 60 percent of baby hummingbirds reach adulthood, most of them taken by predators. Once hatched, however, the babies are much less likely to be caught.

By the time the nestlings are ready to be fledged, the nest has been stretched to its brink. If the mother bird has not been meticulous enough in her house building, it could break, which is potentially fatal for her young. Of course, severe weather can weaken even the best construction.

After the chicks are ready to venture from the nest, their mother will continue to feed them until they have learned to feed themselves. While it varies from species to species, most chicks are ready to take a first clumsy flight after three weeks, at which time the mother may chase them away, thrusting her chicks into the solitary life of the hummingbird.

ABOVE: This male tufted coquette (Lophornis ornatus) *in flight shows off his telltale orange neck plumes. They appear dotted black, but when the light is right, the dotted tips turn a dazzling emerald green. He sometimes makes a nasal buzzing sound with these neck feathers during courtship and territorial displays.*

The Long and the Short of It

The bee hummingbird of Cuba, the smallest bird in the world, is tiny enough to perch on the eraser of a pencil, while the giant hummingbird of the lower altitudes of the Andes, is the world's largest hummingbird. At up to nine inches in length, it is about the size of a swift and nearly seven inches longer than the bee hummingbird.

With more than 340 species, this is only a hint of the vast diversity of hummingbirds, which come in reds, purples, greens, blues, golds, and rusty browns. There are a variety of tail lengths and sizes, as well as straight and curved bills, some short and some astoundingly long. While the United States and Canada boast beautiful hummingbirds, the most unusual species, with astonishing crests and tails, exist south of the border. Nearly half of the known species live within ten degrees of either side of the equator.

The crests worn by the males of some species are the height of nature's creativity, as well as its sense of humor. The tufted coquette of Trinidad and Venezuela has red feathers that stick out on the top of its head like a punk rock haircut, while the tufts extending from its cheeks are spotted.

In southern South America, the black-breasted plovercrest of forest habitats has a long black pointed

ABOVE: The spectacular male black-breasted plovercrest (Stephanoxis lalandi) of Brazil and Argentina has a wispy black crest extending from the back of his head, violet-blue forehead, crown, neck and chest, and a prominent white spot behind each eye.

BELOW: The male festive coquette (Lophornis chalybeus) of Argentina, Brazil, and Bolivia is well-known for his unusual green cheek feathers with white tips. He also has a white horizontal stripe on his rump.

crest extending from the head, while the festive coquette of the savannahs has spectacular green cheek tufts with white tips.

Amazingly, some hummingbirds carry long tail feathers that they must balance in flight, a particularly impressive feat while hovering. The most famous example is the male streamertail, which is only found in Jamaica. There appears to be no other purpose for the tail except sheer beauty, as traveling with such baggage is a huge energy expense. The two long tail feathers are crossed most of the time, but come slightly apart for fleeting moments during flight. Because its tail is so dramatic and actually hums along with its wings, the bird's attractive neck crest and red bill are often overlooked.

In the case of the red-tailed comet of the high Andes, both males and females have long forked red tails with black tips.

ABOVE: The bill of the green-fronted lancebill (Doryfera ludovicae) may not be as extensive as the sword-billed, but its unusually long, thin beak is impressive just the same. This lancebill displays the blue of his tail as he hovers at epiphytic heath in a Costa Rican cloudforest.

The most spectacular tails of all, however, are the "racket tails." The male booted racket-tail of the Andes has two long, thin tail feathers with a round "racket" at the bottom of each. Besides fluffy feather boots hanging over his feet, he has exceptionally loud humming wings.

When it comes to bill length and shape, evolution has stepped in to reduce competition. Some birds have evolved bills that are capable of feeding from only a few types of flowers. The sword-billed hummingbird of the Andes has a decided advantage over the opposition with the longest bill of all hummingbirds. At $4^{1}/_{2}$ inches in length, its bill is almost as long as its body, which requires that the bill be pointed upward in order to balance while perching. Not surprisingly, the sword-billed is a trapliner, which can feed from long tubular flowers that no other bird can reach.

Also of the Andes, the purple-backed thornbill has the shortest bill of all hummingbirds and can feed only from the shallowest of flowers. Its entire length including its bill is only 3¼ inches, compared to the 10-inch length of the sword-billed hummingbird.

The prize for the most unusual bill goes to the white-tipped sicklebill of the forests of Costa Rica and northern Peru. Its crescent-shaped bill makes hovering complicated, so its feet are stronger than most species, allowing it to perch on the curved flowers from which it feeds.

The current number of known hummingbird species was not compiled until the mid-1900s. New subspecies are still being discovered in Latin America. Subspecies are birds that were thought to be the same as another but are found, after further study, to bear slight differences.

PREVIOUS PAGE:
The streamertail exists only
on the island of Jamaica
(Trochilus polytmus),
and the male is famous for
his long streamer-like tail
feathers. Note his bright
red bill, black cap, and
black crest protruding
from the back of his neck.
His breast is a shimmering
emerald green.

ABOVE: The male booted racket-tail (Ocreatus underwoodii) *of the northern Andes Mountains has two astonishing round feather structures at the bottom of his tail and white feather boots hanging over his feet.*

BELOW: The sword-billed hummingbird (Ensifera ensifera), *also of the northern Andes Mountains, wins the prize for the longest bill among hummingbirds. It must sit with its bill pointed upward in order to balance its weight.*

The majority of species in South America do not migrate, as their habitats offer a temperate climate year round, although a small number of such species do migrate very short distances. On the other hand, the only species in North America that do not migrate are the Anna's and Allen's hummingbirds. It is estimated that over five billion hummingbirds migrate every year, and the most impressive travelers are the ruby-throated and rufous hummingbirds of North America.

After gorging for several days to almost double their weight, these birds take off on journeys twice per year that would seem impossibly long for such a small animal. The storage of body fat allows the birds to fly as high as 10,000 feet and up to 500 miles at a time, even through the night without eating or sleeping. Sometimes, they fly until their energy is almost depleted, making periodic stops along the way for a few days to replenish their storage. Ruby-throated hummingbirds have been known

SPECIES FACTS:

- If hummingbirds come in sizes from small to extra small, then the bee hummingbird, at only two inches, would certainly be extra *extra* small. Compare this with the "giant" hummingbird at a whopping nine inches.

- Hummingbirds also come in different styles, as some sport elaborate feather structures such as head and neck tufts or long racket tails.

- Bill sizes and shapes vary greatly as well, from the sword-billed hummingbird with a $4\frac{1}{2}$-inch bill to the purple-backed thornbill with a $\frac{1}{5}$-inch bill.

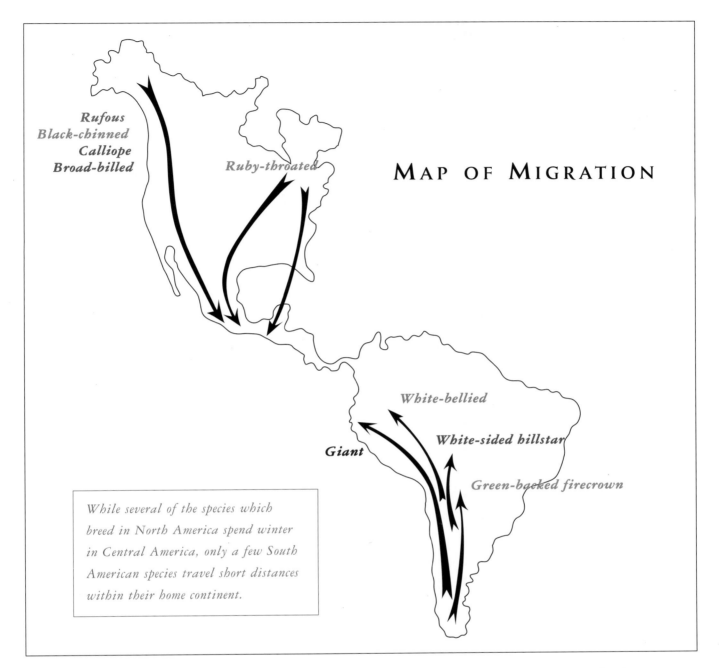

MAP OF MIGRATION

Rufous
Black-chinned
Calliope
Broad-billed

Ruby-throated

White-bellied

White-sided hillstar

Giant

Green-backed firecrown

While several of the species which breed in North America spend winter in Central America, only a few South American species travel short distances within their home continent.

to fly from the Yucatan Peninsula to the Gulf coast in a single night. Many of them cross the Gulf of Mexico nonstop on 60 wingbeats per second. Oil workers on the Gulf maintain nectar feeders to ensure as many birds as possible survive the journey, as it is believed large numbers never complete it.

Hummingbirds do not flock, but rather migrate alone. Therefore, individual birds will fly different routes to their summer or winter locations. Since juvenile hummers are not taught which direction or route to fly, they set out using an inner navigation system that science has yet to comprehend. The theory is that hormones triggered by changes in daylight hours tell them when to migrate, but how they know what route to take is unknown.

Some ruby-throated hummingbirds travel more than 2,000 miles per year

between summering in the eastern United States and wintering in Central America. Depending upon their final destination, they will set out in early spring, arriving in the northeastern United States in April.

Most hummingbirds in the western United States migrate along the Pacific coast. It is the feisty and highly territorial rufous hummingbird, however, that is the champion voyager. In a stretch from Mexico to Alaska, it will travel as much as 2,500 miles each season, perhaps with the help of tailwinds.

The high risks of migration would seem to make it wholly impractical, but it affords the birds less competition in northerly climates during the summer breeding season when flowers and insects are abundant there. In the more temperate wintering territories, there are many year round species with which to share food.

The sixteen beloved species that breed in the United States are spread throughout the continent and Alaska. Anna's and Allen's hummingbirds frequent the coasts of California, while the Costa's hummingbird is the most prevalent in the desert. In the Rocky Mountains, the most commonly seen species are the broad-tailed and Calliope

PREVIOUS PAGE:
The extreme curvature of the
beak of the white-tipped
sicklebill (Eutoxeres aquila)
can make feeding complicated,
but this one manages nicely
while perched on a heliconia
in the Costa Rican rain-
forest. Males and females
look alike and have streaks
on the throat and belly.

hummingbirds. The buff-bellied hummingbird is found in Texas and Louisiana, and the ruby-throated hummingbird is sighted east of the Great Plains in summer. In the western United States, look for the black-chinned and rufous humming-birds in fall and spring. The rufous is the only species in the northwestern United States, Alaska and western Canada in summer. In the hummer abundant southwest, you could be blessed with Lucifer, magnificent, blue-throated, violet-crowned, buff-bellied, broad-billed, and white-eared hummingbirds.

Vagrant or accidental species are those which arrive in areas beyond their normal migratory habitat. Most vagrants in the United States

LEFT: A male green-crowned brilliant (Heliodoxa jacula) *feeds from a bromeliad in a Costa Rican cloud-forest. Note the green crown, white spot behind the eye, and forked tail.*

are seen in southern Florida. Some of these species include the green-breasted mango, Xantus's hummingbird, beryline hummingbird, cinnamon hummingbird, plain-capped starthroat, Bahama woodstar, bumblebee hummingbird, and Cuban emerald.

The information that we have about migration and species habitat is largely due to the work of a few licensed hummingbird banders. Still, only a small number of birds can be caught in soft mist nets and fitted with numbered bands, making it very difficult to determine populations. To make it even more complicated, many banded birds are never seen again. However, a good number of migrating birds return to the same feeding grounds every year, sometimes even on the very same day as the previous year.

Banding hummingbirds is a painstaking and delicate business. The band is made of aluminum and is minute compared to the size of a penny. It must be filed absolutely smooth, or it can cut the bird's leg. Once on the bird, it has to be closed with special pliers small enough not to pinch. The bird can only be safely handled and prevented from feeding for a few moments, just long enough to apply the tiny band, weigh the bird, and take a few measurements.

Perhaps with additional studies, scientists will have a better idea how long hummingbirds live. The estimate is three to five years, which is actually a long life for such a diminutive animal. In captivity, they can live more than ten years, with one captive female Planalto hermit recorded at 14 years old.

PART TWO:

Hummingbirds in Our Midst

Attracting hummingbirds to your backyard is not difficult, but it does require dedication, as you must be willing to either plant the right kinds of flowers or keep your feeders filled and clean.

The perfect backyard hummingbird experience, of course, is the natural garden. It is especially helpful to plant flowers that bloom at different times during the year so that the birds always have plenty of food. Flowers should be planted where they can be protected from excessive wind by a building or fence. Scout your yard for hornet's nests, and be sure to keep feeders and hummingbird flowers well away from them. Hornets are not only likely to steal nectar, but will aggressively fight hummingbirds for it and may even eat nestlings. Be sure to never use pesticides in a hummingbird garden, as they kill the insects which the birds need for protein.

Just a few of the trees and plants preferred by hummingbirds are: azalea, begonia, bird of paradise, bromeliads, butterfly bush, cannas, cardinal flower, columbine, coral bells, cosmos, crab apple, delphinium, foxglove, fuchsia, geranium, hollyhocks, honeysuckle, impatiens, Indian

PREVIOUS PAGE: A
broad-billed hummingbird
(Cynanthus latirostris) of
southwestern North America
sips from a bottle feeder.

ABOVE: A green hermit
(Phaethornis guy) fans
his tail, showing off his two
long white center tail
feathers, as he samples sugar
water from a saucer feeder.

OPPOSITE PAGE:
Fire lily (Cyrtanthus
vallota) is just one of
the many flowers you can
plant to attract humming-
birds to your garden.

paintbrush, lilac, lily, monkeyflower, morning glory, nasturtium, redbud, rose of Sharon, tree tobacco, and wisteria. Check with your local nursery to find out which plants will best grow in your region.

Even if you plan to attract hummers with sugar water feeders, it helps to have a few of their favorite flowers in your garden. If you want lots of hummingbirds, put up several feeders in different locations to reduce competition. With patience, any type of feeder will eventually attract them, although it may take two seasons before they visit with any regularity. There are upside down bottle feeders and saucer-shaped feeders with red flower-shaped holes made of glass or plastic. Red is the most common color used, but it isn't

TREES THAT HUMMINGBIRDS LOVE:

California and Red Buckeye
Catalpa
Crab Apple
Eucalyptus
Hawthorn
Horse Chestnut
Locust
Mimosa
Redbud
Silk Oak
Tree Tobacco
Tulip Tree

PLANTS THAT HUMMINGBIRDS LOVE:

Aloe Vera	Delphinium	
Azalea	Foxglove	
Bee Balm	Fuchsia	
Begonia	Geranium	Morning Glory
Bird of Paradise	Hibiscus	Nasturtium
Bromeliads	Hollyhocks	Ocotillo
Butterfly Bush	Honeysuckle	Penstemon
Cannas	Impatiens	Petunia
Cardinal Flower	Indian Paintbrush	Pink Powder Puff
Chuparosa	Lantana	Rose of Sharon
Columbine	Lilac	Snapdragon
Coral Bells	Lily	Trumpet Creeper
Cosmos	Monkeyflower	Wisteria

absolutely necessary. Bottle shaped feeders sometimes drip, and the spilled nectar attracts insects. Because the feeding holes in saucer feeders face upward, it is best to get one with a roof to prevent rain from diluting the sugar water.

While hummingbirds do not perch at flowers, a feeder equipped with a perch saves them energy. Since feeders contain more nectar than the average flower, the birds hover for longer periods of time at feeders. The downside of perches is that other nectar-eating birds may take advantage. If this becomes a problem, be sure to put up a hummingbird feeder or two without perches to reduce competition. Obviously, if you wish to photograph hummers in flight, you will want at least one feeder without perches.

The most important consideration in choosing a feeder, however, is how easy it is to clean. Hanging hummingbird feeders is a commitment, as cleaning them regularly is absolutely necessary to avoid fermentation of the sugar water, which can encourage deadly fungi growth. Plus, hummingbirds may simply go elsewhere if the water becomes dirty. Every three to four days, or when the water is cloudy, empty the feeder of any remaining sugar water. If you live in an excessively hot climate, the nectar must be changed more frequently. Flush the feeder with hot water, and use a bottle brush if necessary. If it requires more cleaning, use a mixture of water and vinegar, but never soap. If black mold is present, you may soak the feeder in mild bleach water. Rinse repeatedly

LEFT: In the tropics, hummingbirds will often feed from the bird of paradise (Strelitzia reginae) *flower.*

OPPOSITE PAGE: Five Anna's (Calypte anna) *hummingbirds share a single saucer feeder. This display of generosity is rarely seen near flowers, which contain less nectar than feeders.*

to remove all of the bleach, and allow it to air dry as much as possible before filling with nectar. The feeders must be up every morning by dawn, or you run the risk of losing your hummingbirds, especially if they're new to your yard. If they have been feeding in your backyard habitually for some time, they will be less likely to give up on you. You may even find one staring at you as you fill the feeder, waiting for you to hang the food within its reach.

Feeders should be placed in areas where they are shielded from the wind and where there are trees, shrubs, vines or clothes lines for perching. If you have hummingbird flowers in your garden, the birds will find the feeders faster if near their natural food sources. If you can place overripe fruit in an area where a swarm of fruit flies will not bother you too much, the flies will attract hummingbirds. With a backyard of both nectar and protein available, it is only a matter of time before hummers will visit.

Be sure to watch your feeders from a safe distance until the birds become accustomed to you, at which time you may slowly approach them. Most people hang their feeders near windows so they can enjoy watching the birds from inside. This is perfectly fine as long as some precautions are taken. A hummingbird may fly into the window by mistake if there are no decals, windsocks, or miniblinds to indicate the window's presence. The hummingbird could also mistake its reflection for a competitor and

BELOW: A bee buzzes near a fiery-throated hummingbird (Panterpe insignis), *as it glistens in the sun in Savegre, Costa Rica.*

LEFT: This long-tailed hermit (Phaethornis superciliosus) *at the Canopy Tower in Panama must sip from the feeders quickly before being chased away by other species. Note the curved bill typical of hermits, as well as the long white tail feathers, black mask, and back wing position. Males and females of this species look the same.*

attack, sustaining a fatal head injury. If this becomes a problem, try attaching pictures of predatory birds to your window.

Avoid placing feeders in an area where cats roam freely, as they are occasionally successful in catching a hummingbird. If you own a predatory cat that spends some of its day outside, simply refrain from putting up bird feeders of any kind, as cats have seriously reduced bird populations in the United States.

Now, how do you make sugar water? It is very easy, and while there are commercial solutions for sale, they are no better than your own solution and may actually spoil more quickly. The vitamins the commercial formulas contain are unnecessary for wild hummingbirds with access to insect protein as well as nectar. The ideal mixture is four parts water to one part white cane sugar. *Never* use brown sugar or honey, as it ferments and is dangerous to birds. Other types of sugar have been tried, but hummers decidedly prefer sucrose, even occasionally rejecting more natural sugars, such as beet sugar. Always boil the water (adding extra to make up for the water that boils away), and remeasure it before mixing in one part sugar. After the sugar dissolves, allow the water to cool completely before filling the feeder. If you make too much, it will keep for a few days in the refrigerator. Never increase the amount of sugar in your homemade nectar. Not only do the birds dislike higher concentrations, but there is evidence that it may damage their livers. *Never* add red food coloring to nectar, as it is unnecessary to attract the birds, and its effect on them is unknown. Distilled water is also not recommended because distilling removes the water's natural mineral content.

Nectar feeders attract bees and ants as well, but some of the newer feeders are equipped with moats or guards that prevent insects from reaching the nectar. Paint any yellow portions of your feeders red, as yellow attracts bees and wasps. Some people use oil or duct tape around the feeder wire to discourage ants. This is not advised because the oil can damage hummingbird feathers, and the duct tape can become stuck to the birds. Bats are also nectar eaters and may raid your feeders during the night. Bear in mind that these animals also pollinate many plants, so think twice before denying them nectar. The problem is that the bats could leave the feeders empty by dawn when the hummers arrive, so what to do about this problem is a matter of personal judgment. If you're an early riser, you have the option of feeding both kinds of animals. Additionally, hummingbird moths raid nectar and are often mistaken for hummers because of the similarity of their flight, even though they're actually larger than some hummingbirds.

If your feeders have been up for a couple of weeks and no birds are visiting, try hanging red ribbon from them, or add orange or red fluorescent tape somewhere on the feeder where the birds do not perch. Just be sure the tape is pressed all the way down. Bear in mind that if the birds frequenting your yard are unfamiliar with the type of feeder hanging there, it may take them a few days to try it. You may suddenly notice fewer birds during some of the summer months, as the

ABOVE: *A female green-crowned brilliant* (Heliodoxa jacula) *takes a sideways sip from a heliconia. Unlike the solid green breast of the male of her species, she has a white breast speckled with green.*

females are breeding and spending most of their time nesting. Still, when your backyard has become an established territory, you can expect migratory species to visit you every summer.

In some southern states, the birds will enjoy your feeders all year. Regardless of your location, however, it is recommended that you leave feeders up all winter unless you live in a very cold climate that could freeze the nectar. Your feeders can be a lifeline for stragglers that are too young or too slim to

migrate south for the winter. If you find a hummingbird wintering in a very cold environment, contact your local Audubon Society or wildlife rescue agency for assistance. Do not attempt to equip your feeders with warming light bulbs without expert help, as you could do more harm than good.

Handling wild birds is illegal and should always be avoided. Contact a wildlife agency if you suspect a bird is injured or ill. If you see a nest with eggs or chicks, don't assume the mother has died or abandoned it. Before calling the authorities, wait at least thirty minutes to see if she returns. Try not to draw so much attention to the nest that you attract a predator's gaze, and abstain from getting too

ABOVE: The very rare hyacinth visorbearer (Augastes scutatus) is endemic to a small area of eastern Brazil and is classified as "near threatened." This female takes a break from her nesting duties. She feeds trapliner style, while the males of her species are territorial.

close, or you could frighten the mother away. Bear in mind, too, that a young fully feathered hummingbird may rest on the ground while learning to fly, appearing injured when it is actually healthy.

If you cannot find a local agency to assist you, you may call the International Wildlife Rehabilitation Council at (707) 864–1761 or the National Wildlife Rehabilitators Association at (320) 259–4086.

STOPPING THE ACTION ON FILM

It wasn't until the 1960s, when camera technology was able to capture rapid hummingbird wings on film, that scientists truly began to grasp the agility of these animals. With faster shutter speeds than our eyes can see, a single wingbeat can now be suspended forever on paper.

For consistent results, professional photographers construct elaborate setups with multiple strobe lights and flash attachments. Obviously, this is too complex for the average amateur photographer.

A point and shoot camera, however, is virtually useless for hummingbird photography. The shutter speeds required necessitate the use of a 35 mm single lens reflex camera or advanced digital camera with a high quality lens and the ability to manually set the shutter speed. A lens that can reach at least 300 mm is preferable, especially in wilder settings. The new lenses, which compensate for camera shake are

especially useful for hand held shots, but can be quite expensive. A tripod will bring best results.

The use of high speed films and flash attachments assist in stopping the action rather than simply recording a blur. However, high-speed films tend to produce grainier prints and cannot be enlarged without loss of quality.

Stay aware of the position of light in relation to the bird, and choose appealing backgrounds whenever possible. When taking photos through a window, be sure to press the lens directly against the glass, or the flash will reflect and appear in the shot. If you take the time to learn as much as you can about photography in general and your equipment specifically, you should eventually be able to get some beautiful hummingbird photos.

ABOVE: This male purple-throated mountain-gem (Lampornis calolaema) *displays his purple gorget while feeding from epiphytic heath in the cloudforest of Costa Rica.*

WHERE TO FIND YOUR FAVORITES

If you are a city dweller with no backyard, there are often bird sanctuaries and parks that attract hummingbirds. In the northeastern United States, ruby-throated hummingbirds can be found in summer even at New York City sanctuaries, such as the Jamaica Bay Wildlife Refuge. Today, many zoos have captive hummingbirds flying freely in aviaries filled with flowers and feeders.

If you are a complete novice, call your local Audubon Society to find out where to find hummingbirds in your area. The Society may even have guided bird watching excursions to get you started. The only essential equipment for bird watching is a good set of binoculars, as hummingbirds often fly quite high and perch in trees against the sun.

PLACES TO WATCH HUMMINGBIRDS:

NORTH AMERICA

Arizona-Sonora Desert Museum
Tucson, Arizona
(520) 883–1380

Borderland Tours
(for U.S. bird watching tours)
Tucson, Arizona
(800) 525–7753

Gila River House
Gila, New Mexico
(505) 525–2383

James San Jacinto Mountain Reserves
Idyllwild, California
(909) 659–3811

Kenedy Foundation Ranch
Sarita, Texas
(800) 757–4470

Santa Rita Lodge Nature Resort
Sahuarita, Arizona
(520) 625–8746

Victor Emanuel Nature Tours (for worldwide tours)
Austin, Texas
(800) 328–VENT

SOUTH AMERICA

Asa Wright Nature Centre
Trinidad
Information from:
Caligo Ventures, Inc.
Armonk, New York
(800) 426–7781

Canopy Tower
Panama
(800) 854–2597

Kapawi Ecolodge
Ecuador
(for a more remote adventure in the most hummingbird-rich country in the world)
Information from: Latin American Expeditions
South Miami, Florida
(888) 368–9929

For resources in your area, contact:
National Audubon Society
700 Broadway
New York, New York 10003
(212) 979–3000

The Nature Conservancy
4245 North Fairfax Drive,
Suite 100
Arlington, VA
22203-1606
(800) 628–6860

ABOVE LEFT: The highly territorial male blue-chested hummingbird (Amazilia amabilis) *in Panama has a blue-violet gorget and green crown which only shine bright in direct sunlight.*

ABOVE RIGHT: From the back, the male blue-chested hummingbird (Amazilia amabilis) *looks quite different as he relaxes his feathers. Note the tiny, tightly-packed feathers of many hues.*

For the ultimate in North American hummingbird watching, the Sonora Desert of Arizona has the most species in summer of any location in North America. Texas is also a great place to find hummingbirds, as is Louisiana.

If exotic hummers are your fantasy, there are many ecolodges throughout Central and South America and the Caribbean, devoted to bird watching. Those that hang feeders, such as the Canopy Tower in Panama, seduce some of the world's most spectacular species so close that your binoculars are superfluous. These lodges range from very easy and comfortable to those only for the most intrepid of travelers. A search on the Internet will yield infinite choices, as well as tours designed specifically for birders.

Ecuador boasts the most hummingbird species with a total of 153, followed by Colombia with 135. Costa Rica is very tourist friendly and extremely popular with birders because its 53 species are more densely concentrated than in any other country. Trinidad, Venezuela, Panama, and Brazil are also popular sites for viewing hummingbirds.

The dream of many a birder is to see every type of hummingbird in a lifetime. However, the time and travel necessary to do so would make it next to impossible. Some species are so uncommon and remote that they are rarely seen by anyone, and some in the Andes Mountains are limited to small habitats at low oxygen altitudes. Still, the list of species seen in a lifetime can be quite extensive if you choose the world's most prolific locales.

HUMMINGBIRDS IN DANGER

Because of their remarkable speed and flying ability, adult hummingbirds are rarely caught by natural predators. Such small morsels are barely an appetizer for any animal of significant size, making it hardly worth the extreme effort of catching one. Still, if an animal is hungry enough and lucky enough, hummingbirds can be caught by hawks, orioles, roadrunners, and other large birds. These birds do, on occasion, purposely bump a hummingbird in flight and nab it while it is recovering. Eggs and chicks, of course, are much more in danger from predators such as snakes, crows, jays, mice, house cats, and even praying mantises. Using spider silk for nest building is occasionally a hazard, as a

BELOW: The stunning male Juan Fernández firecrown (Sephanoides fernandensis) *is one of the most endangered hummingbird species in the world.*

hummingbird stealing silk or insects can get caught in the spider web and eaten by its resident. This is an ironic twist, as hummers also eat small spiders.

Unless a flower is especially seductive, a hummingbird will avoid putting its head all the way inside while feeding. Since sharp eyesight is one of its best defenses against predators, this would put the bird too much at risk.

ABOVE: This male violet sabrewing (Campylopterus hemileucurus) *shines with color and shows off his white outer tail feathers as he hovers at a ginger flower in a cloudforest of Costa Rica. He is one of the larger hummingbirds and has been pictured on the stamps of several Central American countries. Like the hermits, the males of this species sing together in leks to attract females.*

Hummingbirds are most at risk when in torpor, however, as it is a tremendously vulnerable state. With energy dropped as low as possible, they cannot recover quickly from a predator's approach.

Severe weather and the difficulty of migration claim many hummingbird lives every year, but humankind poses the greatest threat. Certain laws do provide a degree of protection. The Migratory Bird Treaty Act of 1918 prohibited killing birds or selling the nests of birds that migrated between Canada and the United States. In the 1970s, Mexico was added to the Act. It wasn't until 1987 that the Convention on International Trade in Endangered Species (CITES) was put in place to protect all hummingbird species. These laws always have opponents, and conservationists must continuously fight to keep them in effect.

Accidental deaths also claim the lives of hummingbirds. The red portions of electrical fences and garage doors have killed confused birds that attempted to feed from them. Covering the red with black paint can rectify this. The most common cause of accidental death in North America, though, is flying into a window. As previously mentioned, decals on windows near feeders or hummingbird flowers help to prevent this hazard.

Like all animals in North America, urban sprawl continues to force hummingbirds to try to find new areas, which may or may not offer the necessary habitat for survival. When flowers are removed for housing, farming or cattle raising, many hummingbird lives are at stake. Because memory sends them back to the same flowers and feeders season after season, if lost food sources are not replaced immediately, hummingbirds can die of starvation within a day. The now popular backyard feeders in America are believed to assist hummingbirds that have lost vital habitat. However, house cats left outside pose a danger to unsuspecting backyard birds. Additionally, even though it has not been proven that insecticides harm hummingbirds directly, spraying certainly kills the insects which provide the birds with vital protein.

As more and more hummingbirds are displaced and move into new territories as vagrants, they sometimes must learn to adapt to harsher climates or perish. They may also find themselves competing with unfamiliar species for food, which can be dangerous to the new arrivals, as well as the residents. Human intervention has caused some species to become more abundant, which may at first sound wonderful. However, as these species migrate south, they bring increased competition to native species. This unnatural change in populations can upset nature's balance beyond what science can measure.

In the tropics of Central and South America, logging and deforestation are the worst threat to the birds. Even hummingbird rich Costa Rica, which has more conservation laws than most Central and South American countries, has seen many of its old growth forests obliterated in the last few decades. Rainforest soil is only useful for farming for a few years, as the soil is dependent upon the decaying plants for nutrients. When the native plants are cleared, the soil quickly loses its ability to sustain any plant life for farming or cattle raising.

A tropical ecosystem consists of an intricate balance and synchrony between all of its plant, insect and animal life. Even the smallest human intervention can upset that balance and cause a domino effect. When a forest is cut, all nectar-bearing flowers, insects, spiders with their webs, and birds that inhabit the forest go with it, not to mention other animals. Besides reducing the numbers of native hummingbirds, lost tropical forests may also cause starvation among migrants that are accustomed to using the area during the winter season or as a rest stop on their way to wintering territory.

Those birds with small habitats or only one or two flowers from which to feed are usually the most in danger of extinction. The very endangered Juan Fernández firecrown *(Sephanoides fernandensis)* lives only on an island called Isla Robinson Crusoe, which is 350 miles off the cold coast of Chile between the southern tip of South America and Antarctica. The turquoise-throated puffleg *(Eriocnemis godini)* of Ecuador is believed to already be extinct.

Approximately 70 species are believed to be either endangered or vulnerable to extinction, with some appearing to have less than 50 live birds remaining in the wild.

THE OTHER MOST ENDANGERED SPECIES:

- black-breasted puffleg *(Eriocnemis nigrivestis)*
- black Inca *(Coeligena prunellei)*
- blue-capped hummingbird *(Eupherusa cyanophrys)*
- Bogota sunangel *(Heliangelus zusii)*
- chestnut-bellied hummingbird *(Amazilia castaneiventris)*
- Chilean woodstar *(Eulidia yarrellii)*
- colorful puffleg *(Eriocnemis mirabilis)*
- Esmeraldas woodstar *(Acestrura berlepschi)*
- gray-bellied comet *(Taphrolesbia griseiventris)*
- Honduran emerald *(Amazilia luciae)*
- hook-billed hermit *(Ramphodon dohrnii)*
- mangrove hummingbird *(Amazilia boucardi)*
- marvelous spatuletail *(Loddigesia mirabilis)*
- royal sunangel *(Heliangelus regalis)*
- Santa Marta sabrewing *(Campylopterus phainopeplus)*
- sapphire-bellied hummingbird *(Lepidopyga lilliae)*
- violet-throated metaltail *(Metallura baroni)*

PART THREE:

Hummingbirds in History and Folklore

Little is known about how hummingbirds evolved through the ages. Because of their small size, no fossils remain to determine how long they have survived on the planet. Some scientists believe they began in the northern Andes of South America, while others theorize they evolved in the tropics and moved north. Scientists agree, however, that their wide range of habitat indicates they have been in existence for a long time.

Linnaeus was the first to publish biological data on hummingbirds, although science of the 1750s did not afford him total accuracy. Europeans first believed hummingbirds had no feet. This explains the name of their avian order in biology, Apodiformes, the prefix of which means "without feet."

European artists began painting the beautiful birds in the early 1800s, although they used stuffed birds as models, since visiting the Americas was a long and expensive journey. Hundreds of thousands of hummingbirds were killed for hat ornaments and other decorations in 19th

ABOVE: The Hummingbirds
and Two Varieties of Orchids
Martin Johnson Heade (1819–1904)
Oil on canvas
Private Collection

century Europe. Some hats sported feathers, while others displayed whole stuffed birds, and there is a record of 12,000 hummingbird skins being sold at a single auction in England. Some species actually became extinct as a result of this trade, which is evidenced by remaining stuffed specimens that are unlike any birds alive today.

Thanks to the Audubon Society and the growing number of conservationists in the early 1900s, the practice of killing hummingbirds for decoration became unpopular. The 1918 Migratory Bird Treaty Act finally saved the hummingbird from this exploitation.

LEGENDS OF LOVE AND VALOR

Native American legends in both North and South America are filled with stories about hummingbirds. Mayan legend says that the hummingbird was the last bird created. Because it was made from leftover, drab feathers, the other birds felt sorry for it and gave it some of their most beautiful parts. The resplendent quetzal offered its iridescent green feathers, the house finch donated its red gorget, and the swallow gave its white tail feathers. The hummingbird of Mayan culture, made colorful by the generosity of other birds, became associated with the sun, which disguised itself as the beautiful bird in order to romance the moon.

Many tribes share this association with love. Hummingbird feathers have been used for generations to make love charms and are said to open the heart. Ancient Mexicans wore stuffed hummingbirds around their necks to attract love and even ground the dried heart of the bird into an aphrodisiac.

Because of their magical flying abilities, hummers have long been connected with the supernatural. Many tribes, especially the Aztecs of Central America, named their gods after hummingbirds and adorned themselves with hummingbird feathers, which they believed could remove curses. The Aztecs also believed that the first flower came into being when the god of music and poetry disguised himself as a hummingbird and made love with a goddess in the underworld.

The Mojave tell the story of a time when people lived under the ground and knew only darkness. It was the hummingbird that ventured to the land of the sun and led the people to the lighted world.

The Chayma people of Trinidad would never harm a hummingbird, as the birds are believed to be the spirits of their ancestors. Hummingbird feathers are used by the Pueblo in a ritual to speed the reincarnation of a deceased newborn child. Because of torpor, the birds' association with death is not surprising. Much like Romeo thought of Juliet, anyone who came across such a bird must have thought it to be dead and later resurrected.

Also not surprising is that these aggressive little birds are forever linked with the warrior. The Aztecs said their slain warriors became hummingbirds in the afterlife, drank nectar in the gardens of paradise, and eventually returned to earth in hummingbird form. Therefore, the birds were believed to be reincarnated warriors who practiced their skills with one another to prepare for fighting the spirit of darkness.

ABOVE: *This ancient sand carving of a humming-bird in the desert of Nazca, Peru is so large that it can only be seen from the air.*

The Taino people of Florida and the Caribbean used their word for hummingbird to refer to their bravest warriors. For the Navajos, the hummingbird remains a symbol of courage, alongside the eagle and the wolf.

The spectacular streamertail of Jamaica, popularly known as the "doctor bird," is still believed to have healing powers.

The Hopi and Zuni Indians called hummers "rainbirds" and believed they were responsible for persuading the gods to bring rain. These tribes painted hummingbirds on their water jars, and the Hopi still include the bird among their sacred kachina dolls. Similar to the Hopi and Zuni, Pueblo Indians have created dances to bring rain, during which they wear hummingbird feathers. Some tribes never tampered with a hummer nest for fear of causing a flood.

The most delightful legend related to rain also comes from the Pueblo, in which the hummingbird obtained its brilliantly colored gorget by flying through a rainbow while in search of rain.

The Nazca people of Peru also painted hummingbirds on their water jars. In an apparent effort to bring rain, their tribute in the desert of Nazca, Peru remains the most

stunning example of the hummingbird in ancient mythology. This giant sand carving has inexplicably survived for 1,500 years. At 300 feet, it is so large that its hummingbird form can only be seen from the air.

Perhaps George-Louis Leclerc, in his "L'histoire naturelle" published in 1775, described hummingbirds best: "Of all animated beings, this is the most elegant in form and the most brilliant in color. The stones and metals polished by art are not comparable to this gem of nature."